Oh God, Oh God, OH GOD!

Supernatural, real-life experiences and
their meaning and significance.

An Autobiography by Elwood G. Watson II

WestBow
PRESS
A DIVISION OF THOMAS NELSON

WestBow Press books may be ordered through booksellers or by contacting:

WestBow Press
A Division of Thomas Nelson
1663 Liberty Drive
Bloomington, IN 47403
www.westbowpress.com
1-(866) 928-1240

Because of the dynamic nature of the Internet, any web addresses or links contained in this book may have changed since publication and may no longer be valid. The views expressed in this work are solely those of the author and do not necessarily reflect the views of the publisher, and the publisher hereby disclaims any responsibility for them.

Any people depicted in stock imagery provided by Thinkstock are models, and such images are being used for illustrative purposes only.

Certain stock imagery © Thinkstock.

ISBN: 978-1-4497-2673-7 (sc)
ISBN: 978-1-4497-2672-0 (e)

Library of Congress Control Number: 2011916693

Printed in the United States of America

WestBow Press rev. date: 11/7/2011

Testify

I love to tell this story
about things from up above,
pertaining to the miraculous,
brought forth by His holy love.

Our Father wants us to know
more about Himself.
He activates His deity;
I've received power myself!

So, dear reader, what you'll hear
are events that really happened.
They're miracles that point the way
to better understanding the Holy, Great I Am.

Elwood Watson
January 2011

"They overcame the enemy
by the blood of the Lamb
and by the word of their testimony"
Rev. 12:11NIV

To Connie Rostosky,
with heartfelt gratitude and much appreciation
for the word processing and the arrangements
of the details of this book.

PREFACE

I am so excited to share with you the amazing history that you now hold in your hands. These are true-life accounts of God's direct intervention in my life. This is all so miraculous that I knew, without a doubt, it just simply had to be shared. What good is a testimony if not shouted from the rooftops to bring witness to the majesty and power of God?

Concerning the title, these are not just vain utterances of our precious Lord's name, but rather an example of the awe that comes from being in His glorious presence. When you are part of a miracle, something that God is doing with you, for you, or around you, the magnitude of being subjected to His power and presence is so stunning, that there are simply no words left to utter other than, "Oh God, oh God, oh God!"

I don't fully understand why all these wonderful things have happened in my life. I know it's not just because I am "Elwood Watson". But, for some reason that I trust He will reveal to me in the future, God saw something "in" me – perhaps the willingness to be bold enough to share it all even at the risk of being mocked – that He could use to reveal Himself to all of us, His beloved creation. God intently desires to be intimate with each and every one of us in such a deep and meaningful way that we would all just come to *expect* His involvement in even the most minute details of our lives.

As you read through the pages of this book, my prayer is that you will come to know, really know, that God truly *is*; and that He, the magnificent, wondrous, all-powerful author of all that was, is and ever will be, desires to be just as intimately acquainted with *you*.

CONTENTS

SHOESTRINGS

I was between five and a half and six years old, living in Dormont, Pennsylvania. I had a little tricycle, and I was just enjoying life as a kid. I had high-top boots in those days, and I was proud of those boots. They had a little pocket on the side where you could carry a penknife. I had all that, and it was just a very peaceful, nice life that I was having as a child.

It just so happened that those days were at the height of the Great Depression. People had nothing. I can remember men occasionally coming to my mother's door, where we lived as a family, knocking on the door, and asking, "Madam, can you spare a crust of bread?" Imagine that! "Can you spare a piece of bread?" I lived through these times and witnessed this even as a small child.

People didn't have much, like clothes and shoes. I, myself, had just one pair of shoes other than my high-top boots – a pair of tennis shoes. My dad had only one pair of shoes. And my mother, just one pair, and maybe a couple of house dresses. That's all she ever had. But with my mother being a fine cook, we were able to eat her lima beans, homemade bread, and foods like that, and survive. It just was the situation, and as a kid, naturally I didn't know that these were destitute times.

My mother was a precious woman. She had actually come to the United States from England when she was only one year old. She had learned many old English lullabies from her own mother.

1

Before I headed out to play my mother would very frequently sit in the old wicker rocking chair, set me on her lap, and in her beautiful alto voice would sing me the following children's tune:

> *Naughty Jack went out to play*
> *in the meadows yesterday.*
> *His mother told him not to go*
> *down by the brook where the rushes grow.*
> *But he did, and he tumbled in,*
> *and he got wet up to his chin.*
> *Such a cold he got in his head;*
> *sneezing makes his face quite red.*
> *Achoo! Achoo! Oh!*

This was her warning for me to not go, myself, into the brook that nestled behind our own home. How precious, my mother.

Okay, so back to my shoes . . . running and playing in the street on concrete, naturally I'd get a hole in the bottom of my little tennis shoes. My mother or dad would then cut out a piece of cardboard and put it inside so I could continue to play.

One day my mother was helping me get dressed, out on the porch putting my little tennis shoes on me. She said, "Oh, these laces are all broken down! I'll have to go in the house and see if I can find another set of shoestrings." So I sat there and waited, and she soon came back out. She said, "I found these shoestrings to replace the ones that are shot in your shoes." She took them out, and as she was restringing my shoes she said, "Now, I know these are going to be a little too long, but we'll tie them in double knots so that when you are running and skipping you won't trip and fall." So she did just that. With caring fingers, she took the old ones out, put in the new shoestrings, and of course they were way too long. She was on her knees as I was sitting down on the front porch and she was tying them into double knots, tightening them up real good to keep the strings from dragging.

I started to play and she went back to her housework. Maybe two hours later – it was late in the morning around 10:30 or 11 o'clock – I looked up and noticed that the sky was getting very black. There was a massive thunderstorm coming! And it just moved right over our neighborhood! You can't tell me God doesn't move in some fantastic ways! All of a sudden, a huge downpour came down.

I ran up on the porch to watch. This was interesting to a little kid, to see this thing. As there was a slight slope to the street, the water was just rushing down the street along the curb. After about five minutes of this downpour, it stopped altogether. The sun started to come out, and I naturally thought, *This is interesting!* I walked out onto the sidewalk, stood above the curb, and looked down onto this water almost a foot deep rushing down the street. Just like any little kid I thought, *Wow, this is really neat!* and I just had to jump in. So I jumped in with both feet! The water was shin deep and I sloshed around a while until it finally all left. Soon the sun came out and I just continued to play.

Naturally, these shoestrings that were tied in double knots had gotten soaked. But, I just continued to play all day long. Around four o'clock in the afternoon my mother came out on the porch and said, "Come on in; it's time for supper. Take off those dirty shoes."

Now, these big double knots had been soaked with water from the storm, and then the sun's heat had caused them to dry and shrink even tighter. It was impossible for human hands to untie these shoestrings! So, I sat down with my little fingers and started digging at these knots. I was sitting there on my hind end, when my mother came up and forced the screen door open and said, "I told you to come in here for supper. Take those shoes off!"

I said, "But I can't get the shoestrings undone. I can't get the shoes off."

She came over and knelt down beside me and worked a bit with her fingers, then finally said, "Well, no one could take these off; I will have to go in the house and get the scissors."

While she was gone into the house I sat back down and tried one more time. You know how your fingers get a little bit sensitive from digging at a huge thing like that? Well, my fingers got sore. I just couldn't get these shoestrings undone! I sat back on my hind end, looked up into the sky, and said, "God, if there is a God in heaven, let these shoestrings become untied and I will forever believe in the power of God!"

I looked down, and all four shoestrings were laid wide open! Instantly! Miraculously! God was right there. How God picks His own! God untied my shoestrings.

My mother came out on the porch with scissors in hand, and she asked, "How did you get those shoestrings undone!? Well, never mind, take those shoes off and come in."

I told this story in World War II to about 4,000 men in a big field during a religious service. They were having testimonies, and I told this story about my shoes. People came up to me afterward and said, "That's really fantastic!" Now that was a genuine miracle. Thus began this amazing journey of life: my hand-in-hand walk with a very involved and ever-present, loving Father God.

Elwood and his little brother sitting on the sidewalk in
front of the porch where the shoestring miracle took place.

MY CONVERSION

I grew up living at 1114 Illinois Avenue in Dormont, Pennsylvania. In those days I would get a quarter a week to put in the bank. At one point I actually had close to $30.00 in that account. I could walk from where we lived, only about two blocks, up to West Liberty Avenue where there was an Isaly's. And I would love to get a Klondike; they were only a nickel then.

I remember my dad came home one time with an extremely sad look on his face. The banks had totally failed. The monies that we had were all gone. We didn't have the bank accounts anymore. That's the way it was in those days; you have no idea the trial of the times.

When I was in first or second grade, my teacher would say to me, "Make sure you get an apple and a glass of milk every day." She was so concerned about the children getting enough nutrition in those tough times. So, getting a healthy snack was the first thing I would try to do when I would get home from school each day.

I know these things may seem a little unusual today, but that's just the way it was when I was a kid. It wasn't uncommon then to walk up the street to get a Klondike, or a penny's worth of candy. There was this one little girl that lived about a block from me. Every time I would walk on that street, she would run out and give me a big hug. We were just little kids and I thought that was so cute.

I always had an awareness of God growing up, although I never really talked to Him. But that day with the shoelaces, God revealed Himself positively to me! From that moment, God already had me. I didn't have to give myself, or seek God. I did not seek God; I already knew He was present and He was real. "You did not choose me, but I chose you and appointed you to go and bear fruit – fruit that will last." John 15:16 NIV

The year 1973 was a tough year; it was a darker time of my life. This was the year of my divorce, and although I wasn't what you would call "depressed," it seemed that I was never truly happy either. I remember one night that I went into downtown Pittsburgh. As I stood on the street corner thinking about my situation, a realization came to me. *The problem with you is that you don't have God in your life!*

As a man, I did not go to church for close to ten years. In those days I would go to work throughout the week, but on the weekends I would stay up late and then sleep until ten or eleven o'clock the next morning. I would never go to church. In fact, the only thought over those years that I ever had in the direction of God was occasionally I would say, "Thank you, God, for life in spite of the pitfalls and tragedies." And that was it! No church. No Sunday school. Nothing like that. I went to Sunday school as a kid, but as a man, nothing.

It was a Saturday evening, and as usual I went to bed late. The next morning was Sunday, January 6, 1974. This is most important because January 6 is considered to be the real birth date of Jesus Christ. The Greek Orthodox Church and the Vatican both recognize January 6 as the birthday of Jesus. So as I said, I went to bed Saturday night and was sleeping away the next morning when all of a sudden – Boom! My head came up off that pillow and I was totally, instantaneously wide awake and superconscious! I was frozen in a position lying on my side with my head up and alert. And I heard the audible voice of God say three words: **"Go to church."** It was commanded with an authority that only God could have.

That really shook me up! I looked at the clock, which read 10:20 a.m. and Church started at 11. I started to hurry. I don't even know if I shaved! But I hurried and ran down the street where the church was, three blocks away. I ran up the steps of the Dormont Presbyterian Church, walked in, and the usher handed me a bulletin.

I walked down the side because I didn't want to sit up front or anything like that. So about halfway down I picked out a pew, chose a spot in the middle of that pew, and sat down. As we started to pray, everybody was gathered together, maybe 400 people or so. It was a pretty good-sized church. Dr. Orr presided then. So I was sitting there and the music started, and I looked at the bulletin and noticed that there would be Communion this day, and the church would all partake of this Communion in unison.

When it was time for Communion, the minister invited the ushers down. They proceeded to the front and got the trays of bread and juice representing the body and blood of Christ. They started passing them from one aisle to another. Finally the trays came down to the aisle where I was sitting. I watched as everyone in my pew took their juice and bread from the trays. As I received the trays, I remember so clearly taking my two fingers and picking up my portion. Everyone got served and the ushers walked back down front. The minister gave the Words of everything pertaining to preceding the taking of Communion. (Communion is more important in our lives than almost everything going on! Sadly, though, it is regarded as happenstance in most churches today. I just wanted to emphasize that this gift of Communion is really important!)

The minister then quoted the Words of Christ saying, "Take and eat this in remembrance of Me." I watched all the arms going up . . . and up into my mouth went the Body of Christ. At the precise, identical second that I touched my tongue to the bread – representative of His body – , immediately I was transposed into the superconscious, spiritual dimension! I didn't know where I was! At the same instant came a beam of energy like a mule-kicking, powerful blow to my head of Divine energy – this power of God zapped me! Out of 400 people, from approximately 60 feet above me this beam precisely pinpointed my mind at that exact moment!

God got me to the church that morning to do this, to be witness to this miracle of Communion.

At the exact second it crashed into my head, inside of my head and my soul there lit up this egg-shaped rock of sin. I knew this was sin. It was harder than petrified marble, rose-pink in color. This "egg," harder than any substance known to man – this, I knew represented the accumulation of sin in the heart of mortal man. There is only one way that it can be destroyed. And this beam of energy was on it!

In the first moments, nothing happened. Then, it was as if God gave the rheostat a little turn to increase the power. I could see the beam of energy right on that egg! As God turned up the power, instantly it developed a giant crack right down the middle! And then on each side of that crack developed more and more cracks, and it began to crumble into smaller and smaller pieces. I saw this as plain as anything that is or ever was, or ever shall be! It kept crumbling into smaller pieces, rose-pink in color, until it became a powder in consistency. Then, in my spiritual eye where I am seeing all of this, that powder poured out of my head! Powder was pouring out on the right side and on the left side of my head. The accumulation of sins, the sins of an entire lifetime – God set me free! God confirmed me! God made me born again at that instant in time!

I came back to my awareness of this world. I practically staggered home. I even experienced a mild headache for about a week. The power of God is so awesome! This was how He transformed me.

As sure as there are millions of people on this earth, and no two are exactly alike in every manner, how varied each person's personal salvation experience must be; perfectly suited for them, hand-selected by the very God who created them and desired from the beginning of all time this very moment of divine adoption. When people hear a testimony like this, I pray that it will simply show just another example of the many different ways that God chooses to work! It is so personal! It is so miraculous!

I went home and entered the kitchen. I just sat there, marveling at what had just happened. It seemed with every breath I became increasingly overwhelmed with an insatiable hunger for the Word of God. I had a Bible and I started reading it with an intense desire. I was like a sponge soaking up what is needed for existence. I pored over the Word of God. I started going to this church, and to that church, to services and Bible studies even as far away as Homestead, ten miles away! I went to all kinds of meetings, any denomination. I just loved going to church and reading the Bible night and day. I wanted to consume myself daily with God. It was as if I couldn't get enough.

This went on for a whole year. Sometimes I would feel drawn to periods of isolating myself to be alone with God. There were many days where people would ask, "Why don't you come to this Bible study with us?" I would simply decline and tell them I was just staying home, basking in the fellowship of God. It was me and God in my apartment. I would ask Him all kinds of question. And God answered. Wait until you hear some of this!

Shortly after my conversion, I asked to meet with Dr. Orr from the Dormont Presbyterian Church. He was always really good about making time to meet with people. As we chatted, I asked him if I had ever told him about my conversion in the church. I shared with him the whole story in detail. When he had heard it all, he leaned all the way over the armrests of his chair and said, "That is utterly fantastic! You are a wealthy man. You don't have to measure your wealth by money or anything. What you have gained is the greatest treasure of all!"

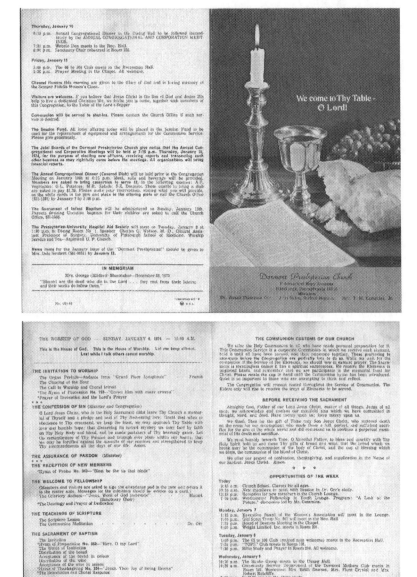

The actual bulletin from the church service of Elwood's conversion.

NIGHTLY SATURATION

For the remainder of that year of 1974 following my conversion, I would go to bed early every night. There was a two-part custom that I had with God nightly. Part one, as I was on my knees, leaning on my mattress, praying and talking to God, the Holy Spirit would come upon me each and every night. My whole body would be ringing and tingling with the power of God all over me. Eventually I would get tired of being on my knees, so I would get into my bed and lay on my back. I would say to God, "Okay, God, now for part two of our conversation!"

In the beginning of my life with God, many times during those nights I would feel a hand on my throat. I am not sure, but I believe that was satanic. I think the enemy was trying to kill me, or maybe just trying to get me to stop talking with God so much! Just like the lesson I recently learned from the bad fall that I took in February of 2010, even though I am a genuine living child of God, we are going to suffer in this world as part of our training. It will be meaningful for us when we get to the next world. The reason we go through this travail now is because we are going to have a position, possibly rulers, in the kingdom to come. We have to be ready to do a good job as a priest or ruler.

Repeatedly, all through each night for some periods of time, the power of the Holy Ghost would physically come upon my body. I don't know if you have ever experienced the Holy Spirit, but it feels like a divine current, this penetrating energy. This would come upon me with such intensity! My whole body would be totally saturated with the divine Spirit of God! My whole mind, body, heart, and soul were flooded with His Spirit; it was so powerful! This went on for several days in this manner, close to a week, and it would go on for hours at a time!

Finally, one night I said, "Dear Holy Spirit, I love what You're doing and I thank You and praise You, God, but You are going to have to lessen the intensity of Your power on me, or it will kill me!" Immediately, from that point on, the intensity of His presence lessened to a really comfortable saturation – still powerful, but not enough to flatten me out!

The power of God continued to come regularly, and one night as I was talking to God, all of a sudden, my voice changed. My voice actually changed! I said, "Oh my, my voice is so beautiful! Thank you, thank you, this is utterly fantastic! I can't believe this is coming out of my mouth! Dear God, I hope this is as pleasing to Your ear as it is to mine." I couldn't believe that my voice actually changed! When we go to heaven and get our new bodies, we are going to get new voices too!

The whole first year of my conversion continued in this same way; I was consumed with the presence of God. Every night I enjoyed deep fellowship with my Creator. I recall one hot summer afternoon as I was lying on my bed, I said, "Oh God, speak to me." And instantaneously I heard, **"You are my son, Elwood."** I can never fully express to you how hearing that voice effected my life. God wants us to fellowship with Him; He wants to commune with us. He wants us to want Him. Don't fear. Just ask.

WHAT ABOUT THESE
TONGUES?

From that time forward, my nights were spent on my knees in fervent prayer. You know when the Holy Spirit comes upon you; anybody who says they don't get tears coming down their face can't be very close to God. Anyway, I would daily converse with God, asking Him all kinds of things. I remember one time I asked, "By the way, God, what about these tongues? What is that? What about these tongues?" And I would try to make up strange sounds, trying to make up a tongue.

This went on for over a week. One night, I was doing the same routine with God. "What about this tongue thing, Lord?" And the Holy Spirit took hold of my tongue – this was not me doing this! I felt a word roll around inside of my mouth. It was my voice in a way, but it was not my voice. It was the Holy Ghost. And here was this word coming out. "Thole, Thole." I was on my knees beside my bed and out came, "Thole, Thole." It just kept replaying over and over in my mind and running through my mouth. I was not doing this with my tongue! The Holy Ghost had taken hold of my tongue and was bringing forth this word.

The next morning I got up extra early and caught the streetcar and went into the County Law Department building where I worked at this time. It was so early that nobody was in the office. They had a very big and extensive library there, so I grabbed the unabridged dictionary and looked up *Thole*. I was coming down the page for *T*, and I knew how to spell it; it was obvious: *T – H – O – L – E*. So I ran my finger down the column, and to my amazement there it was! Thole! I dragged my finger to the right side where the definition was, and it read, "Archaic Hebrew and archaic Greek meaning patience." I jumped up and praised God out loud for giving me one word in tongues, and it was a real word!

I was so happy with that. I went home that night after work, and I dropped to my knees in praise and gratitude. Before I knew what was happening, the Holy Spirit again got hold of my tongue and out poured a whole voluminous discord in tongues! At first I was sort of practicing. I could speed up, slow down. Sometimes it was so fast it was like a computer!

My son, David, who was attending The Culinary Institute of America in Hyde Park, New York at that time, happened to be home from college that week. He would sleep in the sunroom in the front of the apartment, and I was in the back in my bedroom. In my excitement I yelled, "Dave, Dave! Come here!" He got up out of bed, excited, wondering what happened, wondering if somebody broke a leg or something.

I said, "Sit down there. Listen to this! *Della aye doho so holyaeeta, eetrabo hoodia.*" I rattled on like that at a really fast speed. I asked him, "Can you make anything out of that?"

He said, "The only thing I can recognize is the word *holy*."

So that was the beginning of that. After a while I had a bit more control. But the most amazing thing about all this is in regard to my good friend Jimmy Roy, who is sadly now deceased. He was Syrian; his whole family came from Lebanon and frequently spoke in their native language of Arabic. I was a county detective in those years, and I was investigating a case in the building next to his used car lot in Braddock. We became really good friends, Jimmy Roy and I. We spent a lot of years together. We would go to dances and other activities, and pal around together a bit. He became the kind of friend that would give his life for you, and vice versa. He was closer to me than a brother.

Now, Jimmy was the kind of guy who is like a comedian, extremely funny. He was a boxer during World War II in the navy, as well. He had a great personality. As a matter of fact, other businesses used to hire him to give motivational speeches, which he did in addition to owning his car lot. He was a dynamic little guy, though a bit on the eccentric side.

Jimmy owned a furniture store as well as the car lot. One day he shared with the guys he worked with the fact that the Bible said that Jesus could walk on water. He said, "If Jesus can walk on water, then I can walk on water!" Just picture it, fifty guys from his neighborhood businesses all following Jimmy walking down the street five blocks to the river! Everyone was following him to see Jimmy Roy walk on the water. As they all lined up on the hillside, Jimmy walked down the bank in his little dynamic way and he started to walk on the water – and almost drowned! He was disappointed to say the least, but it never dampened his spirit.

One time, Jimmy invited me to have breakfast with him at the Howard Johnson's on the Boulevard of the Allies toward Oakland. I arrived at 10:00 a.m. and Jimmy was already there waiting for me. Being later in the morning, there were no other customers in the restaurant at that time, just me and Jimmy and a couple of the workers. We sat at the counter that morning and put our order in. Just as a gag, right after he placed his order, he turned on his stool to face me and started talking to me in a language that I didn't know. It was Arabic, his native language. He just rattled off to me in fun for a little bit. I turned to him and addressed him in my newfound language – in tongues.

As I started to speak in tongues, he leaned back on his stool looking at me in awe and said, "Oh! You said in perfect Arabic 'Everything is beautiful'! Have you been going to the Berlitz school of languages? Where did you learn how to speak Arabic like that?"

I answered, "I don't know." He relaxed a little.

Then he came on again in another dissertation in Arabic, talking to me, even though I didn't know what he was saying. When he was done, I turned to him and I spoke to him again in tongues. He startled backward, practically falling off of his stool this time and frantically said, "Don't say that! Don't say that! My mother used to say that to me when I was a little kid. You just cursed the devil in perfect Arabic, even with all the guttural intonations of the Arabic language!" I know this language was from the Holy Spirit, as I have never been taught any other language. Who knows, maybe I will be an interpreter *(chuckle)*. But seriously, it was God given, and there was a message in it for Jimmy, too!

Just an important side note to add to all this: when God teaches you something, there is no mistaking where it comes from. In other words, I have had these experiences that I am sharing with you. And when I share them with you, it is like God is repeating the lesson over and over and over again into my heart, body, mind, and soul until I totally understand and have been saturated with the point that He wants to make. When God puts things together, there are no question marks.

Every night I enjoyed praying in my new language with the Lord. I remember one night thinking, "Wouldn't it be awful to lose this gift?" Don't you know, from that point on I couldn't do it! I couldn't speak or even pray in tongues. This went on for the next few weeks. Finally, Christmas Eve rolled around, and in my prayer time with God I said, "I wish there was a gift that I could give to You, God." My gift of tongues was instantly restored! It was so nice of God to give it back to me! I was so overjoyed.

I have often wondered why the gift of tongues stopped. Perhaps it was to show me the reality of His closeness. Perhaps it was so that I would never again take the gift for granted. But looking back, I now see that the gift was restored *after* I had asked what gift I could give to the Father to express my gratitude for all He had done for me. Perhaps, then, this gift is double-edged, bringing blessing to the giver as well as the recipient of the gift. It is, after all, intimate communication with the Father. Can mankind, with all our flawed and wicked ways, somehow "bless" our Creator? This makes me ponder in awe the ways of our God.

SEEING THE FACE OF JESUS

It was the beginning of March of 1974. In the months following my conversion, I had an insatiable hunger for the Word and the things of God. I spent most of my time talking constantly to God. Every night I would be on my knees right beside my bed talking to God. This was my routine, day after day, night after night, just communing with my God.

I was talking to God one night when all of a sudden, right in the middle of my conversation with God, I was interrupted – stopped – and out of my mouth with a voice that didn't really sound like my own (but it was) came the words, "Oh, I would like to see the Lord Jesus."

My head popped up and I was startled. I couldn't understand this. Why would a mere man like myself say something like that? I did not voluntarily say that! That was the Holy Ghost that pulled that out of me. "Oh, I would like to see the Lord Jesus." This may seem a bit odd, but I have to share with you the details of this.

So, with my head popped up I said, "Oh God, please forgive me that a mere man would even entertain these thoughts of seeing you!" And I went back to my prayers. A couple of minutes later, the same thing happened again! "Oh, I would like to see the Lord Jesus."

This really shook me up! Why was I saying that? Again I prayed, "Forgive me, God; this is a terrible thing – that a man is wanting to see you."

This went on and repeated itself several more times throughout the entire night. Thus began this pattern! Now during the daytime, while I would be at work, or walking down the street to lunch, or in my office at the law department, out would come the words, "Oh, I would like to see the Lord Jesus."

After several days, I was starting to get used to this. Day after day this went on. Even in the nighttime, in the middle of the night in the Spirit would come, "Oh, I would like to see the Lord Jesus." By now I had sort of tapered off asking for forgiveness. I knew this was an unusual thing that was happening, but I was resigned that I was going to have to live with this and had begun to adjust to this. "Oh, I would like to see the Lord Jesus." I could be eating my lunch in the cafeteria downtown, or in my sleep in the Spirit; dozens of times during each day, and especially while I was praying, it would come out of me, "Oh, I would like to see the Lord Jesus."

This went on for a period of about five or six days. Then on Friday afternoon while I was writing a brief at the office, I suddenly became tremendously tired. This was very unusual for me on a Friday afternoon around two o'clock. It was so severe that I had to put my pen down. I knew that I was in no condition to work. So I decided that I would have to go home. I went to the cabinet and put my scarf on and my winter hat and coat.

My car was in the parking lot right next door. I got in my car with this weight of exhaustion and tiredness still on me. It wasn't enough to knock me out, but it was close! As I was driving home, I got to Banksville Road and actually had to lean and hold onto the spokes of the steering wheel in order to hold myself up enough to see where I was going – I was that tired!

I finally got up to Broadway in Dormont, to my apartment building. I pulled my car into a parking space at the curb, somewhat askew. I struggled out of my car, got to my front door and opened that, and was barely able to walk up the three flights to my apartment. I put my key in the door and entered in, slamming the door shut behind me. With my hat, scarf, and coat still on I walked about fifteen feet down the hall to my bedroom, and there was my bed. I literally threw myself across the bed, and the last thing that I remember of this world was looking down where my hat had tumbled off onto the hardwood floor.

Instantly I was transposed into a superconscious state, into a supernatural spiritual dimension – immediately and totally! In an instant I was in this condition. I didn't know where I was. But in the Spirit I saw something coming from beyond a "veil" that I somehow knew separated our natural world from the spiritual world. It was a face, and as it passed through the veil, the veil disappeared. Here was this beautiful face, this beautiful head! Not even an arm's distance away! And we were looking at each other!

I was looking at this face and I was permitted to study every aspect of this face. I looked at the beautiful nose, and the chin. The skin was a Mediterranean light bronze color. I looked up at the hair. It was beautiful hair, perfectly parted down the middle and gently waving, not hanging down, just to the nape of the neck as if this person had been to a master hairdresser – not one hair out of place! It was beautiful! Dark brown in color with gentle waves coming down, it was simply a perfect hairdo. I was overcome and marveling at the beauty before me. Then I lowered my eyes a little bit, studying the skin all the time, and came to the eyebrows. They were straight across in the same dark brown color as the hair. Beautiful!

And then, last but not least, I looked into those deep, beautiful eyes. Holiness! Perfection! God! Nothing in all of creation could possibly match this level of beauty! I was looking deep into these eyes, and this was after several minutes of studying this beautiful face. In the Spirit, out loud, I could hear my own voice, "Who is it? Who is it?"

I heard the voice of God reply, **"This is the Lord Jesus."**

If you lined up ten thousand men I could still pick Him out of the crowd, this beautiful face forever seared to my memory. At that minute my own face was taken off of my head and was superimposed over the face of Christ Lord Jesus, and my face blended in and out several times with the face of the Lord Jesus. This was as becoming one with Him. What a marvelous thing!

That ended it. I lifted my head and was back on earth, in this dimension. There are hardly words to express what I felt as I rose from the bed. Euphoric! The heaviness and exhaustion had lifted. It was unbelievable that God would bless me in this fashion. What a gift! The statement "Oh, I would like to see the Lord Jesus" never again came out of my mouth. What I realized from this was that this is the way God wants to teach us, His people! His royal priesthood! God wants us to experience Him, to be open to Him, to function in this way: His way. What a gift!

Muse on our Maker

Methinks Thou art the Mighty King,
great Lord, Master of everything.
Most fortunate one am I,
blessed by Thee until I die.

My soul uplifted sees Thee on thine throne;
You are looking down, calling me Your own.
I've heard thine beautiful, holy voice;
You've announced my sonship; I now rejoice.

Now, dear brethren, prepare yourselves;
destroy the sin in which you delve.
Soon you'll be a ruling saint;
there is no room for the slightest taint.

Look forward to attaining purity of heart,
and you'll see our God from the very start.
There is a degree of happiness that will come your way:
it's "freedom from sin" and it will make your day.

Now enters the Holy Ghost bringing wondrous gifts.
He helps us do the right thing; no longer we'll be adrift.
Then He teaches us to speak in other tongues;
we will remember, then, the love songs that we've sung.

Methinks now my spirit is forever one with Thee;
it's now and continuous throughout eternity.
The hour is late, and I'm going to my bed,
looking forward to the visions that will come into my head.

Elwood Watson
August 2010

TREASURES – AND APPLAUSE –IN HEAVEN

One late evening following my conversion, my dear Lebanese friend, Jimmy Roy, another acquaintance, Bill Scott, and myself decided to go out to the Marriott in Greentree for a night out. A band was playing away and the mood was festive. I don't abide in drinking at all, but my friends were enjoying a beer as we sat in the booth. No matter what was happening around me, I was expounding on the wonders of our Creator, all about God and all about what was mentioned in the Word about Him. It was just flowing out of me, and it went on for several hours like this. I was sharing story upon story from the Bible. Jimmy would get so excited that he would even remind me of still other stories to tell Bill, who was at this time yet unsaved.

So there we were, going back and forth, telling these wonderful stories of truth, and the band was playing away in the background. Where we were really wasn't a good scene, it was a party scene, but I was still talking about God. As I said, this went on for a couple of hours when I finally took a slight pause toward the end. Jimmy just slid down in his seat after hearing about God for all this time, took a deep breath, and said, "I have never felt so good!"

Just after midnight we decided to leave. We walked out to the parking lot, got into my car, and we all went home. It was around 1:15 a.m. when I finally got ready to sleep and plopped into my bed.

All of a sudden I was transposed into a supernatural, superconscious, spiritual dimension, similar to what I had experienced at my conversion. I was totally out of this world! God did this! In the Spirit I saw myself on a platform, something like the top of an elevator. It was as real as looking at someone sitting across from me right now!

The platform started to rise up into the air; just like an elevator it started going up – faster and faster at supersonic speed! Above me I saw dark grey clouds parting as I raced through them at warp speed! This high-speed ascent lasted for several minutes. (That, by the way, makes me realize one thing: heaven is a great distance away!) The platform seemed to pick up speed as it went on. I was acutely aware of everything around me. I could even hear something similar to faint engine sounds, and a sort of shifting of gears as the speed changed. Four or five minutes passed of this climbing at the speed of light!

Suddenly the platform stopped. I looked above me and it looked like I was at the bottom of a well. I knew I was looking into the kingdom of heaven from a much lower level. I saw a twenty-five to thirty foot diameter viewing area where others could see down. It was a large perimeter where I saw all these witnesses who watched the conversation in the Marriott! They were looking down at me, and they were all clapping and cheering about what I had preached on. I realized I was looking up into heaven and hearing the applause of the saints and angels!

Then I saw a mound of treasure right in the center of the opening, the center of this viewing area from heaven. In my estimation it appeared to be approximately three tons of beautiful sapphires, emeralds and gems that heaven is full of! Here was this big pile of this beautiful treasure, beautiful diamonds and sapphires, beyond beauty and description. This, I knew, represented building your treasures in heaven. These "treasures" are *real* treasures for your own private sanctuary. They are real! This is what awaits!

Heaven's Dance

I'm going to dance the polka
when I enter the Pearly Gate.
Saints and angels will all join in
and help me celebrate.

I've conquered sinful ways and death;
I'm praising Him with every breath.
Just listen to that polka band
cheering brethren hand in hand.

Suddenly everyone is looking
over across the room;
it's Lord Jesus, and He's smiling–
He hears the polka tune.

Now we are all together
and we are one with Him;
just gaze upon that holy face
surrounded by the Cherubim.

In unison on our knees we fall;
thank God He's there whenever we call.

Elwood Watson
12/2009

DELIVERED FROM AN
ADDICTION

I thoroughly enjoyed smoking cigars, Camel unfiltered cigarettes, and tobacco pipes for many years. Over those years I had acquired a very nice collection of a half-dozen elegant pipes that I proudly displayed on a fancy rack in my living room. The mahogany pipe rack was grouped together with a beautiful crystal ashtray on a table right beside the chair where I would watch TV. Several times the thoughts had crossed my mind of whether or not this smoking was a good thing to do. But, I didn't pay any attention to the urge to consider these thoughts; instead I just fluffed it off.

One Saturday afternoon I was sitting in my living room chair getting ready to watch a football game on TV. All of a sudden, I just had to turn to the side and look at my pipe rack, with a pipe still in the ashtray. I willed myself to turn back to watch the TV, but then something turned my head again, and I looked back at the pipe in the ashtray with a little more intensity. Again, I determined to look back to the game on TV, until finally I just had to look at that pipe display once again, and this time I really felt *compelled* to study this pipe rack and the ashtray! It was the Holy Ghost that was coming upon me, making me look down at this "shrine." I again looked down at that one pipe that was in the ashtray. I picked it up and looked down into the bowl of that pipe, and I truly felt as if I were looking down a little peephole into hell itself! I couldn't turn my head away; I just kept staring into that pipe bowl.

As I gazed, I started to get shaky and a bit nervous as the power of the Holy Ghost came upon me stronger and stronger. This is the way He works; this is the way God does things. It got so that I started to hate looking upon these pipes, and the pipe rack and ashtray.

Finally, I got so shaken by the power of the Holy Ghost turning me off on smoking that I jumped up beside the chair and grabbed the pipe rack in one hand and the crystal ashtray in the other. I ran through my house, past the kitchen, and out the back fire escape (three stories high), and I heaved them both into the air, down into the garbage dumpster below! I have never smoked since.

How God works, even on the little things in our lives. I never really thought of this smoking as a sin. But then I had to give it some thought, and you know, I just could never picture any of the saints or angels of heaven walking down the streets of gold with a big old smoking cigar sticking out of their mouths. It just doesn't seem to fit! While we are down here, we are, after all, in training for heaven. We are to be ready, oriented, while we are still here on earth. God gives us miracles and lessons now that will even carry over into all of eternity.

THE THREE ANGELS

It was the summer of 1974. I was just going through my normal day when out of the clear blue sky I heard the words come out of my mouth, "Oh, I would like to see an angel." Wow! This was just like the pattern of the past when I would suddenly exclaim, "Oh, I would like to see the Lord Jesus." Only this time, I didn't get bent out of shape. I was a bit startled that this statement came out of me. "Oh, I would like to see an angel." I would perhaps be at a prayer meeting or a Bible study and we would touch on the topic of angels. But here I was, just walking down the street, again in the same pattern as before, out of my lips in the Spirit would come, "Oh, I would like to see an angel." I realized that I had started to accept this phenomenon. This is how God teaches us. He repeats this by way of the Holy Ghost. "Oh, I would like to see an angel." Nighttime, in the middle of the night, on my knees, in the Spirit, all different times of the day...perhaps a dozen times throughout the day...out would come, "Oh, I would like to see an angel." Strangely enough, I got used to this.

It was a hot August afternoon following a previous week of this ongoing prompting. "Oh, I would like to see an angel." I realized this was the last day of the Pittsburgh Art Festival and that I hadn't yet had the chance to go and see the displays. So, I decided to walk down to the festival from my office next to the courthouse in order to go look at the beautiful pictures on display. I came to the small footbridge that crosses over the Boulevard of the Allies. This footbridge had a nice stainless steel handrail that spanned all the way across it to prevent people from falling into the traffic below. As I got to this bridge, I heard some very loud, obnoxious, irritating music coming from some township high school marching band approximately 50 yards away through these giant 12-foot speakers. It was bad. The music was blasting so loud that it was practically deafening!

I leaned on the railing, watching this band, uncomfortably hot and sweaty in my wool sport jacket. I thought how obnoxious it was to demonstrate music in this fashion. They didn't even have rhythm! I was truly annoyed as I leaned my arms on the rail.

Suddenly, I heard a voice in my ear, "What is that?" In my annoyance I snapped back, "That's some kind of lousy high school marching band..." My voice trailed off into barely a calm whisper as I turned and saw three beings. One was in the middle with broad shoulders, wearing a suit and tie and white shirt. I noticed there wasn't a bead of sweat on him! He had blonde curly hair and beautiful blue eyes, all loving. He was sent for this mission! Angels are sent. He was sent so that I could see angels. As he smiled warmly with love, he reached up and touched his own ear and said, "It's alright. I can't hear it anyway."

As he was standing there with me staring at him, I was transfixed! On either side of him were two lesser angels of slighter build. They were looking over my shoulder towards the band playing the music, and they seemed a little bit apprehensive. I wouldn't call them fearful, but they seemed as if perhaps they had never been on earth before. As they were looking at the band, the center being looking at me, all three of them simultaneously started to walk backwards away from me, all the while never losing their gaze. I wanted to go with them more than anything in this world! Inside of me, right in the core of my being, what I somehow knew to be my spiritual essence, seemingly about the size of a fist, fiercely rolled around the center of my abdomen trying to break out to go with them!! My spiritual man wanted to go with them. But yet, my feet seemed cemented to the center of this earth. My flesh was simply unable to go with them even though my spiritual longing to do so was overwhelming! They continued to back away from me about 10-12 feet; all three of them now gazing and warmly smiling at me with immeasurable love. Then suddenly, they disappeared right before my eyes! I knew, once again, God had answered a desire of my heart. God so very much longs to reveal Himself to us. Just be open, just ask, just believe!

TheWonder of it All

I was a new arrival here in Heaven,
and decided to take a walk.
Just wanted to look around
and met angels who wanted to talk.

They told me of places of wondrous beauty
as together we strolled along.
The pathway led down to a river
and we could hear a holy song.

It was the official choir of the Kingdom
singing over the River of Life;
coming forth from the Throne of God
like a perfect loving wife.

The golden waters were hypnotic;
I just had to get right in.
Making my way to the middle,
Oh, what a wonderful swim!

It was a pleasure doing the backstroke
In rhythm with the Holy Choir up there.
I smiled and looked up to God,
"We are the perfect pair"

Elwood Watson
March 2010

WHY GOD CREATED MAN

*"You therefore, beloved, knowing this beforehand, take care
that you are not carried away with the error of lawless people
and lose your own stability.
But grow in the grace and knowledge of our Lord and Savior
Jesus Christ.
To him be the glory both now and to the day of eternity.
Amen."*
II Peter 3:17,18 ESV

Oh the miracles that took place in my Dormont apartment! I was
even allowed to see the face of the Lord Jesus there! Is there anything
He would withhold?

I had a big dining room with a large table where I would sit and
study my Bible. So much fellowship took place there with God. So
many conversations, so much teaching all the time, many things!
So many hours, each day spent in His presence, learning of Him
through His Word. Many times people would ask, "Won't you come
with us to this Bible study?" But at this time my steadfast answer
would always remain, "I am fellowshipping with God right now."

It was a hot day, and after several hours of study I thought I would
take a little a break. I had a daybed right there in that big room, so I
stretched out there to relax in the presence of God Almighty. Being
so encompassed with His glorious presence, as I laid there, tears ran

down my face and in total awe and love I asked, "Oh God, reveal to me one of Your hidden mysteries." I no sooner said that when God pierced my thoughts with an undeniable revelation, and I knew the entire picture of why God created man, in an instant! If I had to read this in a book, what was behind God creating man and the purpose of it all, I would probably have to spend an hour or two to read it. But God revealed it instantaneously! God told me personally why He created mankind on this earth. This is just another way that He works. Mysteriously! Wonderfully!

In the beginning there was the heavenly host with Lucifer and Gabriel and all the arch angels and all the celestial beings that existed. There was a falling out: the Lucifer rebellion. God excommunicated Lucifer from the kingdom of heaven because he wanted to take over God's position, perform miracles, and basically become God. So he was cast out of the realm of heaven. God sent him to the earth, and there would be his domain.

Lucifer asked God about the fate of all of his friends, the angels that might want to go with him. God replied that any of the angels that wanted to follow were allowed to go with Lucifer. One-third of the heavenly host joined Lucifer. Think of it. Now there is a vacuum; there is a void left behind in heaven by the departed angels and Lucifer, who are now confined to earth. God elected to deal with this on the level of His creation. He wasn't going to do a big thing. He was going to bring this about according to God's plan, to His will in this situation.

God has created all things. He cannot lose anything that He, Himself, has created. But now, one-third of this creation is gone out of heaven. God created man on the earth. God snatches the souls of different human beings on this earth saved through Christ and takes them to heaven. God elects and takes them all from earth to go to heaven for one reason: to fulfill that which was lost, to replace that which was lost.

God is a God of the complete work, of wholeness, of completeness and of order. God created mankind to replace that which was initially lost in the kingdom of God – that one-third of the angels that departed with Lucifer are being replaced by mankind. That is why God created man; to replace that which He had already created. God takes man who is in the muck and mire of depravity of this earth with the evil influences, and it is just like He grabs these human beings and shakes the mud off of their heads, all the dirt and the depravity, and He takes them to heaven, snatched from the grip of Lucifer.

The scenario is this: when the time comes, when the exact proportion, the exact equation, the exact amount of spiritual power that was lost with the fall of the angels, the instant that void is replaced by the souls of men, there is no longer a need for this world. That will be the end of this world. That is when Jesus will come back and there will be no more of anything. When the time comes that the spiritual power and essence of mankind replaces that which was lost in the kingdom of God, when that balance – not a couple of souls more or a couple of souls less, but an exact amount of spiritual power that was initially lost, exact to the nth degree – when that is equalized, that is the end of the world, that is the end of creation. Mystery solved.

About one month after this revelation gift was bestowed upon me, I received a divine confirmation. I was attending the Greater Pittsburgh Charismatic Conference at Duquesne University. There were approximately 15,000 people there from all over the country. This was a daily occurrence for a solid week – morning, afternoon and night. There were many famous speakers and it was a wonderful charismatic conference. I signed up for the whole week. I went to all different kinds of classes throughout those seven days. At lunchtime each day, close to one thousand people would congregate out on the big lawn, and they would gather into groups of twelve to fifteen people per circle.

So, one day I thought I would go over and sit in one of these circles of people. As I looked throughout the crowd, I noticed all the seats in each circle were full. But finally I noticed one seat open, so

I went over to that group and asked if the seat was taken. It wasn't, so I sat down with the brothers and sisters in that circle.

Perhaps fifteen to twenty minutes after I had sat down in that one vacant spot, I felt a tap on my shoulder. I turned and looked upon a man that I had never seen before. He said, "I don't know why, but God told me to give you this." He handed me a page torn out from a publication from a monastery in the upper regions of Canada, where he had been. He was moved to give this to me! I had never seen him before, and he had never seen me before.

When I read it I realized it was the exact details, a repeat, of what was just revealed to me concerning the reason why God created man. This was written down by the monks in a monastery. They had the same revelation, probably around the same time, and they put it in their monthly publication. You will see a copy of this torn page on the next page.

Isn't it utterly fantastic how God teaches us? There is no mistake. He confirms it! He repeats things over and over so that they become totally embedded in our essence of mind, body, heart, and soul. When He teaches you something, it is for real! It sticks with you forever. You don't have to re-read it, or re-play it; it just becomes a part of you. Truth is inseparable.

OUR TEACHERS IN THE SCHOOL OF PRAISE

By Richard Weiss

Although there is no mention of angels in the story of creation, these messengers of God appear frequently in the Bible. From the early chapters of Genesis to the final verses of the Apocalypse, they are very busily involved in man's world as they guard, guide, announce, warn, and rescue. They are perfectly obedient servants of the Most High God.

Angels are first mentioned after the Fall of our first parents from their gifted, preternatural state. They are the sword-bearing guardians of the tree of life which fallen man could no longer reach.

Scripture takes the existence of angels for granted. The inspired human authors seem simply to assume that God works in the world of fallen mankind through mediators. In the Old Testament they often appear as ordinary men. In the book of Tobias, for example, the angel Raphael comes into the life of young Tobias to be his companion and escort on the way to Media (Tob.5:5), and his teacher in avoiding the snares of an evil spirit (Tob.6:8).

Our English word, angel, comes from the Greek word "angellos" which means "a messenger." The angel Gabriel brought instruction and discernment to Daniel during his captivity in Babylon (Dan.9: 9:21). The same book mentions Michael as the special guardian of God's people (Dan.10:21). While on his way to Haran, Jacob dreamed that he saw a ladder stretching from earth into heaven which was a stairway for God's angels to go up and come down((Gen.28:12).

And when they are not bringing messages to people on earth, the angels are filling God's heavenly court with praise (Isa.6:1-3).

Angels appear in the New Testament too, the most memorable story being the Annunciation (Luke 1:26). An angel also appeared to Zachary to announce the birth of John, to Joseph to calm his doubts about Mary's pregnancy (Matt.1:20), to shepherds near Bethlehem when Christ was born (Lk.2:8-14), and again to Joseph to warn him of Herod (Mat.2:13).

Traditional teaching of the Church about angels tells us that they are God's creatures, bodiless spirits, and guardians of mankind. Those angels who chose to serve God have made a permanent choice which can never fail or waver. They have been raised to a supernatural state and like Christian man they possess sanctifying grace. The elect of mankind are destined through Christ to take the place of those angels who chose to disobey God, and who have lost their place in heaven.

We have much to learn about praising the Lord from our big brothers, the angels. Instead of letting satan and his fallen angels have the spot-light' they seem to be asking for these days, let's praise God for his good angels, and thank Him for the great multitude of heavenly hosts who sing of his glory.

The torn page from the monks publication confirming why God created mankind.

THE VISIONS

As you already know, following my conversion of January 6, 1974, for almost a full year I was on a "spiritual high." It was unbelievable. Night and day I was with God. During these "high" times, during my half sleep, in my spiritual state every night I was with God, fellowshipping with the Holy Ghost. God would grant me visions, one after the other. For close to a year all these wondrous things were happening all the time, night and day. Although I would be in this spiritual state, I was yet totally conscious and seeing everything. It was not like dreaming, and it was not like being unconscious. In fact, I felt extremely aware and ultra-conscious of all that was being presented to me. For close to a year all these wondrous things were happening all the time, night and day.

PLANTING SEEDS

On these typical nights I went into a type of spiritual dimension, and I was allowed to see things happening in the next dimension. One night I saw, coming through space, two demons being chased by three angels. They came right down to where I was lying. The demons were a little bit ahead of the angels and then they stopped right in my presence. They looked like little Buddhas. These angels and demons at this particular time transposed themselves into a very small state and I was able to actually see them in me, in what I knew to be my soul.

The demons pulled out some shovels and they started digging for something in my soul. I somehow knew that they were digging a hole in my soul to plant a seed of evil. Just as they were really starting to dig, the angels came onto the scene, and then the demons with their fat little bellies and their diabolical laughter suddenly stopped in the middle of their digging and took off. Two of the angels continued chasing them and there was a big battle. But one angel in particular stayed behind, and he repaired what they had been digging. Whatever was in there, this angel dug it out, destroyed it, and then covered the area all back up again so that it was normal.

That was a situation that I found to be really interesting: to actually see them in action. This confirmed to me that there truly is spiritual warfare going on all the time, right now, all around us, everywhere in the next dimension.

AN UNWELCOME VISITOR

The visions God gave me in the Spirit covered the entire gamut of everything that is, good or evil. One night in the Spirit I clearly saw this throne coming through space, and on that throne was Lucifer. Satan himself was on that throne! He was sailing through space and he stopped approximately fifty feet away from where I was.

It was so apparent to me that he cannot be in more than one place at any moment in time. But there he was on that throne. He came to see me! Why? I don't know. As he was approaching me on his throne I could see that he was wearing a gaudy, island-style headdress. He stopped and looked at me, and I just looked right back at him wondering what he was doing there. For some reason he wanted to see me, perhaps to identify me, but I got a look at him, too. This was a very important thing that stuck with me.

A REAL PLACE

God wants us to be aware of all truth, for it will help us in the last days. How many people wonder, "Is there really a hell?" Another night in my bed, again in the Spirit, God was lowering me down deep inside the earth. There were these big mountains down there. There was one particular very steep mountain where I saw a type of manhole cover vertical in the side of this mountain. I saw the lid taken off this round hole, and I had to get on my knees to peer inside. I suddenly realized that I was leaning down actually looking into hell.

I was permitted to look down into the abyss of hell for approximately twenty to thirty seconds. If people could experience what hell was like, whew! I could see and hear and feel and sense that the torture there is unbelievable! If people could witness this, what I witnessed in this real and horrific place, they would find the nearest gigantic cross and they would be flat on their face forever so that they don't ever go there. And sadly, a lot of people are going there. It is a horrible place! I can so clearly remember the feeling of that torture. There couldn't be more pain and suffering. Excruciating!

This reality affected me so deeply, to the extent that I want to share it with everybody. It isn't easy to overcome the sin factors in one's life, but one glimpse of the reality of hell has kept me in a state of repentance, and even more, a state of gratitude for the grace of God. I can't thank God enough for Jesus.

SINKING SAND

In this vision I saw myself walking. As I took each step I would turn behind me and look and see all the earth disappear. It was gone! It looked as if I was going to get swallowed up into that bottomless pit. Every time I took a step, the ground behind me would crumble away! This happened probably ten or fifteen times. There was nothing behind; it was void! What had been earth was now gone!

I finally came to a railing, similar to a fence. I grabbed hold of it and turned around facing the drop-off, and I saw the last big chunk of the earth fall away into the bottomless pit. As I was standing there witnessing all of this, all of a sudden from above me came down a pole. I knew it to be divine, holy energy. It came down right beside me, the bottom of it hovering only a few inches off the ground from where I was standing. I could feel, see, and sense the divine, holy God energy in this pole. Then I heard a voice say, **"The Lord has need of thee."** How humbling to think that the Lord of the universe and of all that is could have need of mere man! But we are all called to be His hands and His feet.

HIDDEN TREASURE

One night as I was in a deep sleep, I suddenly found myself awake in another dimension, taken out of my body up into the air. I was lifted up very high and found myself soaring through the air in a horizontal fashion heading north east. I looked down and actually recognized places that I had been before, certain cities and towns in Pennsylvania. I then recognized what I knew to be Allentown, and knew that I was close to the border of New Jersey.

After quite some time of continuing this type of travel, I came to an abrupt stop, still suspended up in the air. I looked down and I saw a beautiful white church surrounded by a perfectly kept, green lawn. Even though the church was so well-kept that it appeared brand new, I knew it was very old. Mysteriously, this church seemed somehow untouched by the elements of time and weather.

As I looked down upon this scene I asked, "What is this? Where am I and why am I here? What am I doing here?" I heard a voice respond out loud, **"This is Nova Scotia."** Not long after hearing that voice, I found myself back in my body, lying once again on my bed, back in this mortal dimension.

Interestingly enough, a short time after this vision, I found myself at a local large-chain bookstore. There was a big table covered with a wide variety of books on clearance sale. There were approximately one hundred and fifty books all lined up with only their bindings visible. I walked over to that table and very haphazardly reached down among all those books and with my forefinger pulled up one, lone book. It turned out to be a history of the Knights Templar. It looked interesting, so I decided to purchase the book.

In reading this book, I learned that the Knights Templar owned their own fleet of ships, and had sailed from the European continent across the North Atlantic, past Iceland, then proceeded southward to the island of Nova Scotia. Over the centuries, the Knights Templar was known to obtain vast quantities of great treasure. The most amazing element of the Knights Templar treasure is believed to be the Holy Grail.

I can't help but believe that these happenings are more than mere coincidence. Was God revealing a hidden mystery to me? One can only wonder.

A VISION OF MONUMENTAL PROPORTIONS

I am constantly amazed every time that I retell this story.

My conversion was January 6, 1974. For many months after that, I just pored over the Bible. I spent almost every waking hour talking to God. I went to every Bible study and prayer meeting I could find. I went to many different churches, basically soaking up every drop of the Word of God I could come in contact with, because now I was saved.

In June of this same year of 1974, I became friends with a good Christian, born-again woman of God who lived two buildings away from me. She worked for U.S. Steel at the time and decided she was going to have a dinner party at her third-story apartment in Dormont. I was invited over for this gathering. It was a fairly large group gathered at her home, thirty to thirty-five people all socializing in her apartment. What a nice group of good, Christian, loving people. The company was great, the food was really wonderful, and the people all seemed to just enjoy mingling with one another.

Most were gathered around the large dining room table sampling all the delicious food. I walked out of the dining room and I entered into the living room where there was a nice, big, comfortable sofa. As I sat there by myself, I watched everyone enjoying their fellowship in the dining room, and I marveled at the beauty of this whole scene. I was smiling to myself and admiring everything that was going on. All of a sudden, I experienced this vision. And this vision is a prophecy also. After all, the Word says to "desire earnestly to prophesy." I Cor. 14:39 NASV

In this instant, I was in a superconscious spiritual state, unaware that I was in this world anymore, totally oblivious to all that was happening around me in the apartment. In this new spiritual world I looked up and I saw the sun blotted out – not black like an eclipse, but there were big splotches like continents over different places on the sun. Even though there was sort of a faded red look to it, I could still sense the intensity of the sun underneath these splotches.

This next part is totally and utterly fantastic and really flattens me out to tell you because I am an old-time horseman. I rode horseback for many years in the past for the county police. Horses play a real role in our life. In the next instant, I could hear hoofbeats, deafening hoofbeats. I saw coming hundreds of thousands of these black horses, three abreast in perfect cadence and harmony. Over one-mile long a procession of them came out of the space from the right in a large arc formation, and I saw them coming, and they went right past me! I didn't actually see myself in the vision at this point yet. But I was observing all of this. The exact precision of the clattering sound of those hundreds of thousands of hooves all hitting the ground at the same time was simply an astounding marvel!

On the back of every one of these black horses were these "beings." Evil beings! Headless! And each one was covered with armor, and even parts of every horse were covered with armor as well. I knew this to be an undeniable element of evil. It took many minutes for them to all pass by before me, as they headed off into oblivion.

In the very next instant, from up above somewhere, I saw two bronze metal masks. I sensed these were the witnesses referred to in the Bible. They looked very similar to drama masks without eyeballs. (I have recently come to find out that *bronze* in the Bible typically is symbolic of judgment.)

The next thing I knew, I was back into the reality of this world, right back in my seat on the sofa at my friend's party. As everyone was preoccupied with their fellowshipping, no one even noticed that I was having this experience in the next room.

Not much later, the party started to break up and everyone left for home. By myself, I walked the two buildings back to my own third-story apartment. I no sooner got into my bed when God once again rendered me into that same superconscious spiritual state! Here I was again, in this new world, witnessing the exact same thing that I witnessed earlier at the party. I noticed that when God wants to make sure I really understand something, He tends to repeat it for me. God knows the limitations and the frailties of our humanity, so He uses repetition to teach us.

This vision was repeated with the exact replication of the first time with one exception. There was the same blotted-out sun, the same hundreds of thousands of armored horses with the same armored, headless riders, just as before. But this time, I saw myself standing there as the horses ran by. I was wearing a robe, a white robe.

After this same hideous and deafening army of evil had almost completely passed me by, finally the last horse came through with its rider. I saw myself take a powerful leap from my standing position, right atop the back of that last horse! With a flurry of my hands, I crumpled up and completely destroyed what was on the back of that horse, and I threw it off into oblivion. Next, I saw myself leap onto the horse in front of that horse as the two bronze masks (witnesses) once again came down from up above.

This vision suggested to me that perhaps my particular role would be in combating and destroying evil in the end times. One can only wonder at the marvels of the ways of God!

GOD'S PATIENCE, AND MY BAPTISM

I continued to fellowship with God all the time, night and day. My big dining room table was just covered with books and Bibles, and God was there! I was able to talk to God and ask Him things, and just like Paul said, "No man taught me anything, but God taught me everything." (Galatians 1:12 paraphrased) That was the same thing with me. God taught me everything through the Bible and through direct contact with Him.

I was wondering about Satan and Lucifer being the same being. I said to God, "You know he's excommunicated from heaven; he has his own evil domain now. Is there any way that these fallen angels and Lucifer could ever come back into heaven?" Immediately the answer was, **"No, they can never go back."**

So, one time God told me, **"I want you to read the book of Acts."** And I fluffed it off. This repeated a couple of times during the day, and still again I didn't obey. Then I heard, **"I told you that I want you to read the book of Acts."** But, I put it off once again, and just only thought about doing it.

That next Saturday evening there was a Clint Eastwood movie coming on TV. I got myself all ready, took my shower, put my pajamas on, and turned on the TV to start to watch this western movie, and I was excited. It no sooner came on when God, with some intensity this time, said to me, **"I told you I want you to read**

the book of Acts!" The command was so firm that I simply had to shut off the program and do what was asked of me.

I grabbed my Bible and started reading the book of Acts. There obviously was a message in there that God wanted me to have. This is the way God does things in our daily lives. So, I read the book of Acts and it was all interesting. I came to chapter 10, verse 47 and when I read it, God hit me with the realization that this is what He wanted me to discover! It was Peter talking in the Bible, saying, "Would we deny water for baptism, even to those who have been born again?" God wants us to be water baptized. It is a wonderful thing! That's what He wanted me to learn right then, that water baptism isn't a suggestion, but rather a command. I thanked God for revealing this to me through His Word.

Very quickly after that I called up the minister of my church and scheduled my own water baptism. It was October 26, 1975. When the day arrived and it was my turn for the actual baptism, I turned to the church congregation and said, "I am getting baptized because God told me to!" Simple as that, I had no other discourse.

This was just one of the many lessons that He was teaching me at that time. This is the way that He does things. He repeats. And He repeats again until we get it. He is patient and long-suffering. And that is the benefit of the whole testimony of all the miracles that have happened in my life. That is how God teaches us. He could simply do things instantaneously with His will; but He elects to deal with things on the level of His creation. He is not wiping out creation; He is using us!

THE HEALINGS

Some years ago, I was seeing a woman at the time, a good, Christian girl. Every Saturday afternoon at 5:00 p.m. I would go down to her house in Canonsburg, and we would watch Kenneth Copeland's ministry program together.

I knew this woman had suffered with severe migraine headaches for over a year. They were the kind that were so excruciatingly painful that she would have to pull all the blinds down and lay in complete darkness for a day or two until the pain subsided. She did suffer so, and from time to time I would see a look of pain come across her face.

On November 5, 1982, I was sitting at one end of the couch and she sat way down on the other. We had just started watching the program, and I saw that look of pain come again over her face. So I asked, "You're in pain right now, aren't you?" and she said, "Yes."

I got up off the sofa, walked across the room, put my hands on her head, and said, "You don't have to stand for this; you don't have to take this! I command this pain to leave you in Jesus' name. You be healed!" That was all, no big discourse.

I went back over and sat on my end of the sofa. In the next moment, she got up out of the seat, and she started walking back and forth across the room. She said, "Oh! There is a big cracking going on inside of my head!" She repeated this statement around four or five more times, and then she sat down. And she never had another migraine from that moment on! God is not moved by our fancy dissertations, but by our simple faith!

—

Another incident comes to mind. It happened in the pew of the church where I had my conversion, even in the same aisle. There was a gentleman sitting there with his family, Ray McCormick, who lived in Virginia Manor in Mt. Lebanon. We all became acquainted, and one Saturday morning there was going to be a men's fellowship. There were about 150 men there that morning for the breakfast fellowship. It was right after the meal when we were all just standing around in groups, talking. I started a conversation with this one man who was a friend of Ray McCormick, who sat right in the same aisle that I did. His name was Lou Davies.

I asked him how he was doing and told him he was looking pretty healthy, and I asked him if he was taking vitamins or something. Lou told me he wasn't, and that in fact he was in quite a bit of pain. I said, "I am really sorry to hear that. What's the matter?"

He held his hand out to me and said, "I have this arthritis in my hand and it is so painful." His hand was all knotted up with big ugly lumps of calcium deposits all over them, totally disfigured.

"Oh my, would you like me to pray for that?" I asked him. He said yes, so together Lou and I went to find a private room to pray, as we didn't want to make a scene or pray in front of all these other men. Well, every room in the church had people in it. We finally went down to the boiler room, opened up the door, and went in there with the big furnace and equipment. I said, "Oh good, there's nobody here." At least it was private.

Lou held out his hand, I put my hand over his hand, and I simply prayed and came against those lumps and prayed for God to heal this hand and deliver him from this arthritis in Jesus' name. That was it. I said, "There." We turned around and went back upstairs.

I prayed for him on a Saturday. The next week, Ray McCormick, who was an expert in air-conditioning in big commercial buildings, had to go to Washington, D.C. to be a consultant on a large commercial project. He took his buddy, Lou, with him; they were like brothers. They were down in Washington, D.C. and Ray was up on this ladder getting into this air conditioning unit and realized he needed his screwdriver set. Lou reached down into the tool kit and handed it up to Ray.

Ray looked down, saw Lou's hand, and in amazement said, "You never could use that hand before! What happened?"

Lou simply replied, "Elwood prayed for me." He even testified in church about this, too.

The next Sunday was the first I had heard of it. Ray saw me come into the church and said, "Oh, there you are, come here. I have been looking for you! Did you hear what happened, did you hear what happened?"

I said, "No, what happened?"

He told me about what happened in Washington, D.C. Lou's hand was completely healed – completely normal.

—

Another recollection of a healing incident occurs to me. I was living over in Brookline at the time, and there was a big snowstorm. One particular Sunday morning I looked out the window and saw that the snow was equal to the height of my car! I had wanted to attend service at Faith Community but with the snow being this deep, I knew I wouldn't be able to get my car out to drive there. So, instead, I decided to walk up to the local United Methodist Church that was only four blocks away. Snow or no snow, I just wanted to go to church.

I walked into the church and asked somebody, "Do you have Sunday School here?"

The usher answered, "Yes, downstairs in the gym."

I walked down to the gym area, and saw at one end of the large room there were around fifteen people sitting around for the class, and one seat was vacant. The class was structured so that there was some teaching, then open discussion and fellowship time. I sat down in the vacant chair and there was a man sitting right next to me. I could see that for some reason this man was very uptight. During the discussion time he shared with the whole group that he was having a terrible time with anxiety.

When the class ended, I got up to leave. As I was walking across the room I heard a voice yelling out, "Oh Mr. Watson, Mr. Watson! Could you hold up a minute?" It was the man with the anxiety.

I answered, "Yes, come on over."

He walked across the gym floor toward me. He stood beside me with noticeable agitation in his manner.

I asked him, "What's the matter?"

He replied, "I've been bothered for months. Something is attacking me and driving me half crazy. I'm really having a bad time; I'm uptight and very nervous all the time!"

I said, "You don't have to stand for that!" And I took my hand and laid it over both of his hands, and I prayed and I came against that evil spirit that was assailing and afflicting this man, in Jesus' name! And we both left.

This is amazing. That night, I once again went into a supernatural spiritual state, and immediately standing in front of me was a snake! I saw this evil thing as clearly and as plainly as the nose on my face. It was as thick as a human being, had a head as big as a basketball, and was exactly as tall as me! It was completely reptilian, a snake, standing on its tail, with markings similar to a python – the size of a human, standing right in front of me trying to intimidate me! I believe because I had prayed for that man and had come against that evil, Satan sent this snake to stand right in front of me and stare me right in the eye to try to come against me.

I immediately took both of my hands and grabbed that snake about a foot below its head to strangle it. I shook it a little and threw it away as if it were just vapor! I thought, "This is something that is nothing more than hot air!"

This meant to me, and I have testified to this, that when evil comes onto you, it is nothing more than a bunch of hot air! It may be evil, it may be mean, but we have the power to destroy evil through Jesus Christ. This is one thing we have to get into our heads as Christians. I have come to learn through all these experiences in my life that there is evil all around us, and these evil beings can see us, and they can come against us and try to affect us. But we have the power, through Jesus Christ, to destroy them!

—

I remember one time I was over visiting my mother in her later years. She was still living at home, as this was before she had to be moved to the nursing home. She had her big Bible on a card table next to her bed, which at this time was in the living room. I sat in the rocking chair diagonally across the room from her and had a wonderful conversation with her about the gift of speaking in tongues.

There was a moment of quiet and I looked over at her. She looked up from her Bible and started speaking in the most beautiful prayer language in her most beautiful voice! It was a moment of pure beauty and joy.

Some years later she suffered a stroke. When the ambulance came to the house, the EMTs assessed her condition and said they believed she had a stroke and advised that she be brought to the hospital right away. They immediately put her in the ambulance and took her to the hospital. In the emergency room she was in critical condition, unconscious but living. They moved her to a private room across from the nurse's station in the special unit for stroke victims. Since she was directly across the hall, the nurses could look into her room and see her at any time.

Her condition was so poor that I was told that she would pass away at any moment and that I might want to consider staying with her at the hospital until her passing. So, I sat in a chair beside her bed where she peacefully lay, her head slightly elevated, her hands at her sides, but with hoses everywhere. I kept a bedside vigil there for almost three full days while she lay in a coma, completely unresponsive.

As I was sitting there, I thought, *I realize what's going to happen. I am going to pray for her.* Up to this point, I hadn't yet prayed for her. I rose up out of my easy chair and went across the room to her bed. I put my hands on her head and said, "Dear God, heal my mother, Norah, in Jesus' name." That's all.

I turned around and I walked back to sit down. Before my hind end could even touch the chair, I looked over at her and both of her eyes popped wide open! That's a healing miracle! From that time forward she started to come out of her coma. She didn't die! She walked a bit, and then lived another several happy years in the nursing home. It's just more proof that our God desires to heal, and He responds to even the simplest of faith.

THE POWER OF THE CROSS

When my youngest son, Bill Watson, was getting married, the ceremony was going to be in the Dormont Presbyterian Church. I got there on this Saturday afternoon perhaps a half hour earlier than everybody else. I was just walking around the church and the church was empty. I walked down the center aisle of the sanctuary, which led down to a podium behind which a large wooden cross was hanging on the wall.

It was relaxing as I slowly wandered around the sanctuary. But, as I walked down the aisle and got closer to the cross, I felt a power like a divine energy coming off of the cross toward me! As I kept walking towards it, the power coming off of the cross grew in intensity against me. I could feel the power coming off of this cross! As I would move closer, it got stronger! So, I stopped and started to walk backward, still facing the cross, and as I backed away further and further, the power lessened until it gradually disappeared.

Praise the Lord! That cross is such a powerful symbol of our God! Don't ever underestimate the power of the cross!

TWO EVIL ATTEMPTS UNDONE!

I remember these two occasions so clearly. God really does protect us!

The first occasion was Christmas Eve in December of 1974 when my son, David, was home on Christmas break from college at The Culinary Institute of America. I was so happy to have him home. It was late and very cold that night as he and I were leaving my apartment to walk over to the midnight service at the church.

There really wasn't anyone else on the street as we walked our way along. We were just chatting and really enjoying each other's company when I suddenly saw this big person, a very large man wearing a long, black trench coat, walking toward us. David saw him as well and sensed something wasn't right. As the large man got closer to us, I noticed my son tensing up a bit, as if he was on guard. This guy was big. When the man got right alongside of us, he pulled open his coat and pulled out a sawed-off shotgun!

Suddenly, the man seemed confused and was really struggling to hold onto the gun. Without reason his hands just opened up, and the gun dropped from his grip and crashed with a loud clatter onto the metal street plate that we happened to be standing over during this encounter. He was stunned and confused. He looked up from the gun to me and asked, "Did you see that?"

I replied, "I didn't see anything." We quickly walked on down to the church and called the police. He was ready to rob us on Christmas Eve! But God had something to say about that!

The second occasion was on a nice summer afternoon. I was going for a walk over to my other son Bill's home, who lived only a few blocks away from me at the time. I walked down on Broadway, crossed over Potomac Avenue, and walked down one street over onto Voelkel Avenue.

A few houses before my son's home, I came to a set of twelve steps that spanned up to the next level, a terrace to a house. Sitting on that terrace on top of that bank I saw a very big collie dog. I didn't think much of it because usually collies are known to be a very friendly dog. But this one wasn't.

As I continued down the sidewalk, as soon as I got even with the steps he was sitting atop the level above me, it was as if something drove that dog. He came charging full speed down that bank—full growl, all teeth, ready to strike! He was coming directly for my leg, mouth open, snarling and growling, ready to attack. He meant business!

As he got mere inches from my leg, he suddenly completely changed! He went right past my leg, tail between his legs, whimpering, cowering, and crying, and he ran yelping all the way down the middle of the street as if all the hounds of hell were chasing him! Something seriously changed his mind. He instantly transformed from being the dominant aggressor to the cowardly, fleeing prey!

God really does protect us!

A MIRACLE ON BANKSVILLE ROAD

It was 1976 and I was on my way to work from Dormont in the old, beat-up Dodge that I owned at that time. It was around 8:15 in the morning.

It's important for you to have an idea of what this road looked like back then. In those days, Banksville Road was a four-lane road, with two lanes going each direction. The four lanes were separated in the center by a hump in the road. If worse came to worse, you could always go up over the hump. Approximately every 200 feet along the dividing hump, there was a steel utility pole embedded in the ground, forty to fifty feet tall. Off the top of each steel utility pole there were two big arcs with lights on them to light up Banksville Road at night.

It was a typical morning rush-hour commute into town, and needless to say, the inbound traffic was bumper to bumper. Even though the traffic was heavy, we were all still moving at the flow of about fifty miles per hour. I was in the center lane, two lanes moving simultaneously.

With no warning, a woman in the right-hand lane changed lanes and barged right into my lane! In order to avoid a catastrophic accident, I quickly swerved my wheel and wound up going right up the dividing hump, flat out at fifty miles per hour straddling the dividing hump of the road!! Immediately in front of me I saw that I was heading full speed toward one of those steel utility poles! A big, heavy-duty pole coming right at me! It all happened in seconds, so quickly that there was no way I could even get my foot off the gas pedal. No question about it, I was dead. I will not be here when I hit that pole.

At that instant, the entire scene went into a different, miraculous dimension! It had to be a spiritual dimension. Everything around me went into this same dimension and I passed right through the pole! As I went through the pole, I swerved the wheel and my car came back down off the hump and back into my lane of traffic. It was a miracle and I saw the whole thing!

The Bible tells us that we are going to suffer in this world. It is part of our training. But, what a situation, to be at the spiritual level we are in, to walk this path of life aware that the God of the universe is walking beside us and is active with us. And God wants us all to share about the miracles we experience. It's the evidence of truth, of His ability, of His love, and it is the weapon to destroy the works of the enemy. God be praised!

THE WHITE OAK INCIDENT

Well prior to the writing of this book, as time was passing by, I asked God how I could possibly remember all the miracles and wonderful things that have happened to me, so I started to write a list of them down. As I was looking over this list, I read *The White Oak Incident*. At first I could not remember what that meant, *The White Oak Incident*. So, I asked the Lord to remind me what it was, and immediately He brought it to my remembrance. God reminded me of this, and it is utterly phenomenal! This is really fantastic and would definitely rate five-star!

This happened before my conversion, going back to when I was around thirty years old. As you may recall, I didn't experience my conversion until I was forty-nine. Even before my conversion, though, spiritual things would happen to me. I was just leading an ordinary life, like everyone else. I was in law enforcement then, a county detective. I was staying at a hotel called the Lincoln Manor in White Oak Borough. I would stay there for days at a time, sometimes weeks at a time, to provide security for the events taking place in the hotel ballroom. It was all free, a place to live and eat and everything. They really treated me well, these people who owned this hotel. They owned a large trucking company as well, and we became very good friends.

During one of my stays, I was sleeping on my side in one of the thirty-five guest rooms of this hotel. (Remember, I was unsaved, not yet converted at this time.) I suddenly became keenly aware of these "beings" that I knew were of another dimension, but they looked just like human beings in every sense of the word. They had the ability to move in the air, through all the material things of this dimension – right through walls, right through buildings, anything!

Two of these beings in particular had moved right through the wall and were up next to the ceiling above me. They were talking back and forth with each other. I couldn't hear what they were saying, but it was clear to my sight that they were engaged in a conversation. They passed over me as if they were going to go right on by, but all of a sudden they stopped, backed up a couple of feet, and started talking about me! In one instant, as they were talking about me, a power came from them and I was frozen stiff as a board in the bed, and I couldn't move. In the next instant, in their power, I was picked up off of the bed into the air (perhaps five to six feet or so) and then I was slammed down into the bed. They did that!

I knew now that I was in really big trouble as they were above me talking about me. It became obvious to me in that moment that these "beings" were indeed evil spirits! At that moment in my fear I said, "Dear Jesus, come into my heart." Jesus was instantly right there! He was present, and all fear was instantly *gone*!

The next thing I knew, Jesus took over the situation. From the bottom of my feet there came a ray of energy from God that was pinkish rust in color, similar to the color of light methylate. This ray of power started at my toes and moved its way up my legs until it covered my entire body. I was completely saturated with what I sensed to be the healing power of God. In the next instant I saw a power come from the fingers of Christ like a three-stranded cable of energy, and it went straight into my heart.

What surprised me in all of this was the realization that these spiritual beings had the power with their will to pick me up and make it so I could not move – I was completely frozen! Every cell in my body was totally rigid, and I simply could not move. I was amazed how they could pick me up and slam me down unmercifully onto the bed on my back. I knew I was in big trouble. But I also knew enough about Jesus from my childhood in Sunday school to have the wisdom to call upon Him. I knew even then, that Christ was the only salvation, the only way out of this terrible situation.

I never forgot what I experienced that night. Nor did I ever forget how the presence of Jesus made me feel from that point forward. I knew I was safe, I knew I was protected, I knew I was His.

SLAIN IN THE SPIRIT

I had attended Faith Community Church for quite a while. They had a big auditorium there. A men's conference was taking place, and the auditorium was filled with around 250 – 300 men for this event. Ed Cole, the famous keynote speaker, was flown in from California. At the conclusion of his message, he invited the men to come down to the front of the auditorium to stand in front of the platform so that he could pray for them individually.

In groups of, say, twenty at a time, the men would come out of the aisles. The ushers helped guide them down to the front for their time of prayer and then helped them return to their seats afterwards. The ushers finally came down to the aisle where I was sitting toward the back of the church. All the fellows in my aisle stood up but me. They all walked down the center aisle and they all lined up down front, standing below the four-foot-high platform.

As Ed Cole started to pray for them, I started to feel this heat coming over me back in the pew. I was resisting this. I wasn't going down there for that. Well, this heat became more and more intense, and the power of God came upon me with such extreme force that I stood up and walked down that center aisle, separated the men toward the end of that row, and stood there to get prayed for. He prayed for each man, just a simple little prayer, and touched each one on the head. He came down past these men, and he stood about six to eight feet from me.

As he was just ready to come over and put his hand on my head to pray for me, he stopped suddenly, lifted his hand up, and said, "I don't know why, but there's a special love of God for you!" Praise the Lord! Then he put his hand on my head and prayed for me, and I felt the indisputable power of the Holy Ghost. Over I went, backward right on the floor, face up! I was genuinely slain in the Spirit. It really is something that brings you closer to God. And there I was, resisting it in the beginning! That is, until the heat of His power convinced me that I needed to do this.

A lot of people will say that being slain in the Spirit is just emotions running wild, but let me tell you something. When you are truly influenced by the power of God, your emotions are powerless! Your emotions have no power to resist submitting to His will. It's not emotions; it's the true and undeniable power of God.

AN INVITATION

This last page typically would be reserved for a fitting conclusion to the book in hand. However, more importantly, this ending is an invitation for you to seek more about the Father.He is the one who set forth these miracles to create a pathway for mere mortals to become more cognizant of His ways.

Take this moment to simply ask Jesus to be the Lord of your life. There's no magic, no trick. It's simple faith that moves the heart of God. Just admit that you have sinned. Ask Him to live in your heart and be your Lord. Then go tell someone about it.

This isn't the end of the story, but just the beginning!

"If then you have been raised with Christ,
seek the things that are above where Christ is,
seated at the right hand of God.
Set your minds on things that are above,
not on things that are on earth."
Colossians 3: 1-2 ESV

The Parade

Soon I will join the big parade
composed of departing mortals.
Together we will leave this planet
and be freed from earthly hurdles.

We will smile at one another
as we take our place in line.
"Glad to see you made it!"
I'll say as we start our climb.

Oh, the marching music is playing
so perfectly by the band;
Can't you just see us strutting
past the reviewing stand?

There is loud applause from the grandstand,
the cheering heard miles away.
It's the welcoming committee,
impressed by our cadence and sway.

The parade is now slowing down;
we can see the Kingdom's gates.
Into the temple we are ushered;
we've become part of this holy state.

Elwood Watson
June 2011

ABOUT THE AUTHOR

Elwood G. Watson II is a man who has devoted his adult life to studying the Word of God, harkening to the voice of God, and seeking after the things of God.

Through the tough times of his childhood during the Great Depression; his teen and young adult years serving in the US Army Air Force during World War II; his years as a uniformed police officer and county detective;, and his later years as a legal investigator for the County Law Department of Allegheny County, Pennsylvania; Elwood has enjoyed an intimate fellowship with the Father and experienced the divine, mysterious, and miraculous direct intervention of Almighty God.

Staying steadfast to his desire to please God by always trying to do the right thing, Elwood is impassioned by a present call of God to share all that the Heavenly Father has done throughout his eighty-seven years for the sole purpose of helping others to understand and truly know their divine Creator.

Currently residing in Bethel Park, Pennsylvania, Elwood is ever-ready, willing and filled with enthusiasm to share his life experiences with his many friends, neighbors, family, and anyone with a hunger to know more about God.